Helping Children See Jesus

ISBN: 978-1-64104-041-9

SIN
Missing the Mark
New Testament Volume 4: Life of Christ Part 4

Author: Ruth B. Greiner
Illustrator: Frances H. Hertzler
Computer Graphic Artist: Ed Olson
Typesetting and Layout: Patricia Pope

© 2018 Bible Visuals International
PO Box 153, Akron, PA 17501-0153
Phone: (717) 859-1131
www.biblevisuals.org

All rights reserved. No part of this publication may be reproduced, stored in a retrieval system or transmitted in any form by any means, electronic, mechanical, photocopy, recording or otherwise, without the prior permission of the publisher, except as provided by USA copyright law.

RELATED ITEMS

To access related items (such as activities, memory verse posters and translated texts) please visit our web store at shop.biblevisuals.org and enter 1004 in the search box on the page.

FREE TEXT DOWNLOAD

To access a FREE printable copy of the teaching text (PDF format) in English or other available languages, enter S1004DL in the search box. Add the item to your cart, and use coupon code XTACSV17 at checkout. Once your order is processed you will receive an email with a link to the free download.

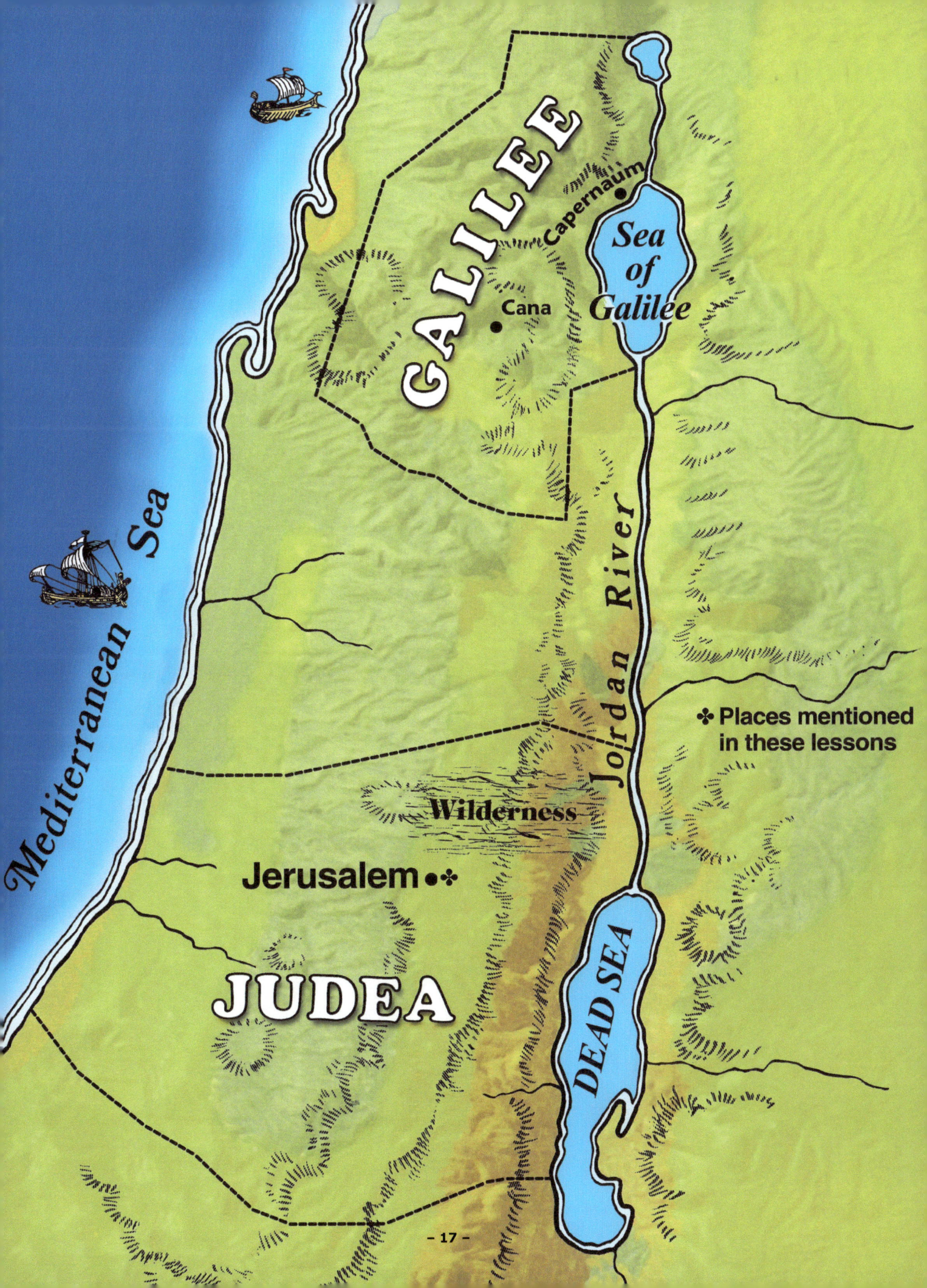

For the wages of sin is **death;** but the gift of God is **eternal life** through Jesus Christ our Lord. Romans 6:23

Lesson 1
JESUS HEALS LEPROSY

Scripture to be studied: Matthew 8:1-4; Mark 1:40-45; Luke 5:12-16

The *aim* of the lesson: To show that the Lord Jesus Christ loves and cares for even the poorest and most needy. Far more wonderful than that: He has power to forgive and cleanse from sin.

What your students should *know*: That leprosy is a reminder of the awfulness of sin.

What your students should *feel*: A desire to have Jesus forgive their sins.

What your students should *do*: Believe that Jesus, the Son of God, died for their sin and receive Him as Saviour.

Lesson outline (for the teacher's and students' notebooks):
1. The lonely leper was doomed to die (Luke 5:12).
2. The leper asks Jesus to heal him (Matthew 8:1-2; Mark 1:40).
3. The Lord Jesus heals the leper (Matthew 8:3; Mark 1:41; Luke 5:13).
4. The leper returns home (Matthew 8:4; Mark 1:42-45; Luke 5:14-16).

The verse to be memorized:

For the wages of sin is death; but the gift of God is eternal life through Jesus Christ our Lord. (Romans 6:23)

> **NOTE TO THE TEACHER**
>
> Let the Lord impress the truths of this lesson upon your heart as you read it in your Bible in three of the Gospels.

THE LESSON

In previous lessons we have learned that the Son of God came to earth to take the punishment for our sin.

This series of lessons has to do with the subject of sin. You may already know a great deal about sin. So suppose you tell me what sin is. (Now, Teacher, ask as many questions as you can, so you will discover what your pupils understand about sin. We will list a few questions. You will think of others.)

1. In the sight of God, what is sin? *(Sin is disobedience to God. Sin is wanting our own way instead of God's way. Sin is missing the mark of the perfection of God. See Romans 3:23; 1 John 5:17.)*
2. If we have done only one wrong thing, are we sinners? *(Yes! See James 2:10.)*
3. How many people have sinned? *(All have sinned. See Romans 3:23.)*
4. What is the one sin that will keep us from receiving everlasting life? *(Not believing in the Lord Jesus as Saviour. See John 3:18.)*
5. What is the punishment for sin? *("The wages of sin is death." That is, to be forever separated from God and all that is good and holy. See Romans 6:23; Ezekiel 18:4b; James 1:15.)*
6. What is the remedy (cure) for sin? *(Believing on the Lord Jesus as the Son of God and receiving Him as Saviour. "The gift of God is eternal life through Jesus Christ our Lord.")*

Sin is an awful thing! And, humanly speaking, there is no possible way to get rid of it. We cannot get rid of our sin by deciding to be good. Cutting off the hand of a thief will not keep him from stealing. How can a person stop lying or cheating or losing his temper? Name any wrong thing you can think of. There is no human way of getting rid of it.

Here are five things to remember about sin:
1. There is no human remedy (cure) for sin.
2. A sinner is lonely.
3. A sinner often loses his friends.
4. His friends may even become afraid of the sinner.
5. Sin separates the sinner from God. "The wages of sin is death." This means to be separated from God forever.

1. THE LONELY LEPER WAS DOOMED TO DIE
Luke 5:12

In His Book (the Bible), God caused a record to be kept of some things that happened to a very sick man long ago. Listen closely. Later, as you think about the man, you will remember the five truths about sin which we have learned today.

Show Illustration #1

"Unclean! Unclean!" The sick man who shouted these words had one of the worst of all diseases–leprosy. In that day long ago, he knew that *no man could heal him*. The white spots on his body would not go away, he knew. Instead they would get worse, becoming ugly sores. This dreadful sickness would finally twist and change his face and body so much, that he would no longer look like himself. He knew this.

The sick man was lonely. He wasn't permitted to go into the synagogue (the place where the Jewish people worshiped God). He was not allowed to stay in his village. (See Leviticus 13:4-6.) *He lost his friends*. No one would ever dare to touch him! It was believed that the one who touched a person who had leprosy would himself get the disease.

His friends were afraid of him. So the sick man had to live alone far away from everyone else. Whenever he walked about he shouted, "Unclean! Unclean!" This was a warning to anyone who might be coming that way.

Slowly–very slowly–the days and nights passed. The man became more sick, more *lonely*–oh, so lonely! Sadly he waited for the day that *he would die*.

> **NOTE TO THE TEACHER**
>
> If your students have Bibles, be sure to have them look up the verses of Scripture. In their notebooks, under the topic of *Sin*, they should write the *references* which are used in answering the questions. Or, if they do not have Bibles, time should be taken for them to write some of the verses so they will have them to refer to.

2. THE LEPER ASKS JESUS TO HEAL HIM
Matthew 8:1-2; Mark 1:40

One day he saw a great crowd of people coming down the mountain. (*Teacher:* Show the mountain on the map on the back cover.) They were following a Man. *How* the sick man knew that the Man was the Lord Jesus Christ, we do not know. He may have heard the Lord Jesus as He spoke to the people. Or perhaps he had seen Him do a miracle.

Show Illustration #2

Crying, "Unclean! Unclean!" the sick man rushed as near to Jesus as he could and worshiped Him. Then, looking up into the kindest, most wonderful face he had ever seen, he whispered, "Lord, if You want to, You can make me clean."

3. THE LORD JESUS HEALS THE LEPER
Matthew 8:3; Mark 1:41; Luke 5:13

Show Illustration #3

Do you know what the Lord Jesus did? He reached out His hand and touched the sick man. He really, truly did. He touched him! Jesus was not afraid of leprosy. Jesus is God's Son.

Ever so kindly the Lord said, "Of course I want you to be well. Be clean!"

4. THE LEPER RETURNS HOME
Matthew 8:4; Mark 1:42-45; Luke 5:14-16

Show Illustration #4

That very instant the man was healed–he was made clean. There was not one sore left–not one tiny white spot. His leprosy was gone!

What a happy man he was! Now he could return to his village. He could *be with his friends.* He could *live with his family. No longer would he be chased away or feared by others. No longer would he be lonely.* He was a happy man–so happy that he wanted everyone to know about the wonderful thing that had happened to him.

He told so many about the miracle the Lord Jesus had done for him, that people crowded around the Son of God wherever He went. Everyone wanted to get to the One who could cure even the dreaded leprosy.

But had the Lord Jesus come simply to heal the sick? No! He came, He said, to give eternal life. That is, life with Him and with God forever and ever. (See John 3:15-18, 36.) Far worse than any sickness is the awfulness of being forever separated from God. The Lord Jesus had come to earth so that all people everywhere would know what God is like. He had come so He could take upon Himself the punishment for sin. He died so that we, by believing in Him and receiving Him as our sin-bearer, might live forever with God.

Like the sick man, you may have the Lord Jesus say to you, "Be clean!" You can have the joy of sin forgiven. Gone will be your fear of death. Far more wonderful than being healed of sickness is to be forgiven of sin. The Lord Jesus alone can forgive sin.

Do you believe that the Lord Jesus is the Son of God? Do you believe He died for your sin? Would you like to ask Him, this moment, to forgive your sin? Will you receive Him as your Saviour?

NOTE TO THE TEACHER

Now that you have studied the lesson, think it through carefully again. Is it perfectly clear that *there is no human remedy for sin*? (In Bible days, there was no cure for leprosy. Because of medicine today, there is a cure for that dread disease. Still, many who are afflicted must live away from family and friends.)

As people who had leprosy were not wanted, so *sinners are often unwanted by others. Sinners are frequently feared by others.* As those with leprosy were lonely, so *a sinner can be the loneliest person in the world.* And *sin eternally separates the sinner from God.* But though "the wages of sin is death . . . the gift of God is eternal life through Jesus Christ our Lord"!

Lesson 2
A SICK MAN–FOUR FRIENDS–AND JESUS

Scripture to be studied: Matthew 9:2-8; Mark 2:1-12; Luke 5:17-26

The *aim* of the lesson: To show your students the absolute necessity of having their sins forgiven.

What your students should *know*: There is only one remedy for sin: believing that the Lord Jesus Christ is the Son of God and receiving Him as Saviour.

What your students should *feel*: A desire to have their sins forgiven.

What your students should *do*:

Unsaved: Believe Jesus Christ is the Son of God and ask Him to forgive their sin.

Saved: Introduce their friends to Jesus.

Lesson outline (for the teacher's and students' notebooks):

1. Four men carry a friend to Jesus (Mark 2:1-3; Luke 5:17-18).
2. They make a way to Jesus (Mark 2:4; Luke 5:19).
3. Jesus forgives the man's sin and heals him (Mark 2:5-11; Luke 5:20-24; Matthew 9:2-6).
4. Forgiven sinners give praise to God (Mark 2:12; Luke 5:25-26; Matthew 9:7-8).

> **NOTE TO THE TEACHER**
>
> The ones you teach may have many needs: food, clothing, good health, or perhaps money. But the greatest need that anyone has is the need of being cleansed from sin. The Lord Jesus Christ alone can pardon and cleanse the heart of the sinner.
>
> Make clear, please, the meaning of the verse for this series and encourage your students to learn it well:
>
> *For the wages of sin is death; but the gift of God is eternal life through Jesus Christ our Lord.* (Romans 6:23)

THE LESSON

"Jesus is here! He has come back to Capernaum!" (*Teacher:* Show Capernaum on map.) The news of the coming of the Lord Jesus spread through the small town and into the country. Many people wanted to see Him. They had probably been waiting for Him to return. Some wanted to hear the wonderful things He had to say: things about God, things about men, things about the future. Others wanted to watch Him perform miracles. They wanted to see His mighty power.

The Scribes and Pharisees also wanted to see Jesus, but for a different reason. The Scribes were teachers of the Law and they were jealous of Jesus. The Pharisees pretended that they were good people and made a big show of their service for God. In their hearts, though, they were very proud. Both the Scribes and the Pharisees wanted to see Jesus, but not because they loved Him. They hated Him! They wanted to find some evil in what He said or did so they could lead the people away from the Son of God.

1. FOUR MEN CARRY A FRIEND TO JESUS
Mark 2:1-3; Luke 5:17-18

Men and women (and children, too, I suspect) crowded into the house in Capernaum–the house where Jesus was. Those who could not get inside, pushed close to the door and windows, hoping to be able to hear what Jesus said.

Show Illustration #5

As they listened, four men tried to squeeze through the crowd. They were carrying on a bed (probably a mat) a man who could not walk. He had a sickness called palsy. Because he never could have gotten there himself, his friends brought him to the Lord Jesus.

Not one person in all that crowd was willing to step aside, not even for a sick man. When the four tried to ease their way through to Jesus, the crowd closed in more tightly, shutting out the men and their sick friend. What could they do? They *had* to get their friend to the only One who could help him.

2. THEY MAKE A WAY TO JESUS
Mark 2:4; Luke 5:19

They could climb the outside steps to the flat roof. But what good would that do? Then they had an idea! The four men twisted and turned to carry their sick friend up the narrow steps to the top of the house.

Show Illustration #6

There they broke away some of the roof tiles. Looking down, they could see the Lord Jesus inside talking to the people.

3. JESUS FORGIVES THE MAN'S SIN AND HEALS HIM
Mark 2:5-11; Luke 5:20-24; Matthew 9:2-6

Show Illustration #7

Then ever so carefully, the men lowered their friend on his mat down through the hole in the roof. Down, down, down he went, right in front of Jesus! Everyone in the room must have been startled. But not one said, "You cannot come here. There is no room for you." No. There *was* room, right next to the Son of God!

The sick man looked up at Jesus. Jesus looked down at the sick man. Because He is God the Son, He knew exactly what was wrong with the man.

Everyone was quiet. What would Jesus do? Would they see a miracle? How would He do it? What would He say? The people could hardly wait to see what would happen.

But the Lord Jesus saw more than the people saw. He saw that the sick man had faith in Him, the Son of God. He saw, too, the faith of the four men who had brought the sick man. Jesus saw how strongly they believed that He would help. What more did the Lord Jesus see? He saw the heart of the sick man. He, the One who knows all things, knew that the sin in the heart of the man was worse than the sickness of the man. Later He Himself said that from within the heart of a man comes all the wrong that a man does: evil thoughts, murders, thefts, pride, foolishness . . . and more. (See Mark 7:20-23.)

– 21 –

It may have been the man's sin that had caused his illness. Not all sickness is the result of sin. No, indeed! But there are many who are sick because of having lived sinful lives. (Some have cancer, for example, from having smoked.) It may be that this man was one whose illness was caused by sin. We do not know. But, like all people everywhere, the man had a sinful heart. And the Lord Jesus saw that.

Instead of healing the sick man, the Lord Jesus said: "Son, your sins are forgiven."

The Scribes and Pharisees, sitting nearby, became angry. They thought, *What wicked things this Jesus speaks! Who can forgive sins but God?*

Because the Son of God knows all things, He knew exactly what those men were thinking. So He answered the Scribes and Pharisees, saying, "Why must you argue like this in your minds? Why does this bother you? Which is easier to say: 'Your sins are forgiven' or 'Get up and walk'?"

The Scribes and Pharisees did not answer. So Jesus continued, "To prove that I, the Son of Man have the right on earth to forgive sins, I say to you (the sick man): Stand up! Take your bed and go home!"

4. FORGIVEN SINNERS GIVE PRAISE TO GOD
Mark 2:12; Luke 5:25-26; Matthew 9:7-8

Show Illustration #8

The man leaped to his feet. Picking up his bed and pushing his way through the amazed crowd, the man went home, praising God.

The people could hardly believe the wonderful thing they had seen. Some, like the healed man, began to praise God. "We have never seen anything like this before," they said.

They would not forget that day. They had seen the Lord Jesus do a miracle. More than that, they had heard the Lord Jesus forgive the man of his sins. If he had been healed and nothing more, he some day would have had to receive the wages of his sin: death. That means that after his life was over, he would have been forever separated from God and from all that is pure and good and holy.

To have any sickness is a sad thing. To be sick because of having sinned is sadder still. But far worse than any sickness is the sin that is in the heart of every man and woman, every boy, every girl. And the same Lord Jesus who forgave the sins of the sick man is waiting to do a miracle in your life: forgive *you* of *your* sin. When you believe that He is truly the Son of God (which He proved by the greatest of all miracles: rising from the dead), when you ask Him for forgiveness of sin, when you invite Him to live in your heart, He gives you His kind of life–eternal life. It is true that "the wages of sin is death." But it is equally true that the "gift of God is eternal life through Jesus Christ our Lord."

God wants to forgive your sin. He waits, this very moment, to give you eternal life. Do you believe that the Lord Jesus Christ is the Son of God? Do you believe He died for your sin? Will you ask Him to forgive your sin and invite Him to live in your heart and life? Will you do it right now?

> **NOTE TO THE TEACHER**
>
> If there are some who want to receive the Lord Jesus as Saviour, lead them to Him, using the ideas given in the inside back cover.
>
> If all of your students are already born into the family of God, you should emphasize that the sick man would never have had his sin forgiven, would never have been healed, if his friends had not brought him to the Saviour. Help those you teach to understand that it is our *responsibility* to bring others to the Son of God.

Lesson 3

JESUS AT THE POOL OF BETHESDA

> **NOTE TO THE TEACHER**
>
> As you study the fifth chapter of John in preparation for this lesson, you will realize how patient, how loving, how gentle the Lord Jesus is.
>
> The man at the Pool of Bethesda was sick, apparently, because of his sin. (See John 5:14.) There was help for him because he turned to the Saviour.
>
> But there was no hope for the Jewish leaders who thought themselves to be as good as, or better than, others. If they had understood how holy God is, they would have seen how sinful they were. They would then not have been too proud to admit they were sinners. They would not have been too proud to believe that the Lord Jesus, the Son of God, is the only One who can forgive sin.
>
> At the end of life, the person who has not received the Saviour will have to receive the wages of sin: death!
>
> By now, this Scripture verse should begin to live to your students:
>
> *For the wages of sin is death; but the gift of God is eternal life through Jesus Christ our Lord.* (Romans 6:23)

Scripture to be studied: John 5

The *aim* of the lesson: To help your students understand that they are sinners.

What your students should *know*: The greatest of all sins is unbelief–not believing in the Lord Jesus as the Son of God and receiving Him as Saviour.

What your students should *feel*: A desire to receive God's gift of eternal life.

What your students should *do*: Believe that Jesus is the Son of God and receive Him as Saviour.

Lesson outline (for the teacher's and students' notebooks):

1. Jesus comes to the sick man (John 5:1-7).
2. Jesus heals the sick man (John 5:8-9).
3. Religious leaders question the man (John 5:10-13).
4. Jesus forgives the man's sin (John 5:14-47).

THE LESSON

We have been learning about sin. In our first lesson in this series, we saw that there is no human remedy (cure) for sin. Sin separates the sinner from God. Next we learned that sometimes sickness is the result of having sinned. But God can and does forgive sin. When a person truly believes that the Lord Jesus Christ is the Son of God and places his trust in Christ, God forgives that person's sin. Today we shall see what happens when people do not believe in the Lord Jesus.

The city of Jerusalem was crowded with people. They had come to celebrate a special Jewish feast and to worship God in the Temple.

However, there were many who could not go to the Temple. They were at the Pool of Bethesda. Some were blind. Others were lame. Still others were paralyzed and could not move. These sick people lay on the porches that were around the pool. They wanted only one thing: to be able to go to the Temple on this important feast day. But they could not. Instead, they stared at the pool, trying not to look away, not even for a moment.

Why did they gaze at the pool? Because at certain times an angel came and stirred up the water in Bethesda Pool. The first person to get into the water after it had been stirred, would be healed. Day after day the sick people waited for the angel to stir the waters. Each wanted to be the first to get into that pool.

1. JESUS COMES TO THE SICK MAN
John 5:1-7

One of the men had been lying on his bed-mat for 38 years. What a long time! He had about given up hope of ever being the first to get into the pool after the waters moved. Always someone got in ahead of him. Still he waited.

Show Illustration #9

On this particular day when the sick man saw a Stranger, he doubtless wondered, *Who is He? What is His name? Why is He here?*

Coming right to him, the Stranger asked, "Would you like to get well?" (*Teacher:* This seems to be an unusual question. But some who had been sick for a long time may have lost the will to be well. Others, we are told, pretended to be sick simply to get money from those who passed.)

"I cannot get well," the sick man said. "I have no one to help me into the pool after the water has moved. I try to get in, but someone is always ahead of me."

2. JESUS HEALS THE SICK MAN
John 5:8-9

The Stranger commanded: "Stand up! Roll up your bed-mat and go home."

In all his 38 sick years, the man had never heard such a command. But the Stranger had spoken so powerfully that there was only one thing for him to do: stand up.

Show Illustration #10

And that is exactly what he did. He was well! He had not even been in the pool! He put his bed-mat on his shoulder and walked, straight and tall, as if he had never been sick.

3. RELIGIOUS LEADERS QUESTION THE MAN
John 5:10-13

Show Illustration #11

Do you suppose the Jewish religious leaders were glad when they saw the man walking? They were not! Rather, they stopped him and said, "It is the Sabbath (the Jewish day of rest). It is wrong for you to carry your bed on the Sabbath."

The man replied, "But the One who made me well told me to pick up my bed and walk."

"Who said such a thing?" the men demanded.

The man could not tell them because he did not know who had healed him. And the Stranger had disappeared. Where He was or who He was, the man did not know.

He hurried to the Temple. At long last, he could worship God and celebrate the feast day.

4. JESUS FORGIVES THE MAN'S SIN
John 5:14-47

Show Illustration #12

There, the One who had healed him, saw him. And again the Stranger spoke to him. "Now you are well," He said. "Do not sin as you did before or something worse may happen to you."

This was when the man learned that the Stranger was the Lord Jesus, the Son of God. At last he understood the reason he had been sick all those years: it had been because he had sinned. Two miracles had happened to him that day: (1) He had been healed of his sickness; (2) He had been forgiven of his sin.

It was wonderful to be able to walk. But it was far more wonderful to be forgiven of his sin. Now he need not dread the awful wages of sin: death. Instead, he had the gift of God: eternal life through Jesus Christ. What a happy, happy man he was!

He rushed to the Jews to tell them that it was the Lord Jesus who had made him well. When the Jews heard that, they tried to kill Jesus. Why? Because He had healed a man on the Sabbath Day! He had forgiven the man of his sin–on the Sabbath Day! For 38 long years the man had been sick because he had sinned. And the Lord Jesus had chosen the Sabbath Day to deliver the man from the effect of his sin. So they tried to kill Him.

Jesus answered them, "My Father works . . . and I work."

Oh, that really made the Jews angry! Not only had the Lord Jesus broken the Sabbath Day (according to the laws which they themselves had made), but He had also said that God was His Father. The Jews had seen the miracle the Lord Jesus had done in healing the man. They had probably seen other miracles He had done. (See John 2, 3, 4.) Others had believed that the Lord Jesus is the Son of God. Why did the Jews not believe? Because they were proud of themselves and of their own laws. And they *refused* to believe the Lord Jesus. They were, perhaps, good men. They were probably religious men. But they were sinful men.

Carefully the Lord Jesus explained that He had been able to perform miracles because He was one with God the Father. He explained that He had the same power as God–power, even, to bring dead people back to life (verse 21). Then He told them that God the Father had appointed Him to be the judge of sinners (verse 22).

Looking into the faces of those religious Jews, Jesus said, "Anyone who listens to My message and believes Him who sent Me, has eternal life and will never come into judgment for his sins, but has already passed out of death into life" (verse 24).

If those men had believed in the Son of God, they would have been sorry that they were proud of themselves and of their self-made religion. Because they did not love God (verse 42), they did not receive His Son. Because they did not believe God or His Son, they were already condemned to death–eternal death. (See John 3:18.) The Lord Jesus had come so that they (and all people everywhere) could have eternal life. He had done many miracles to help them understand that He is the Son of God. If they had believed Him, if they had received Him as their Saviour from sin, they would have received His gift of eternal life. Instead of going God's way, they chose their own sinful way. And the wages of sin is death!

No matter how bad or how good you are, God sees you as a sinner, condemned to eternal death. But the Lord Jesus is waiting this moment to forgive you. If you will receive Him as Saviour, He will give you His gift of eternal life. He died so that you need not die and be forever separated from God. Do you believe that Jesus is the Son of God? Will you receive Him as your Saviour from sin right now?

NOTE TO THE TEACHER
Pray earnestly that your students will understand that the greatest of all sins is *unbelief*–not believing in the Lord Jesus as the Son of God and receiving Him as Saviour. As you pray, the Holy Spirit will speak to the hearts of those you teach.

Lesson 4
SIN AND ITS WAGES

NOTE TO THE TEACHER
In this series we have been discussing the *fact* of sin, the *meaning* of sin, and the *effects* of sin. Our students must learn what sin is. But they must also understand the consequences of sin. God hates sin and He will punish sin.

Because no one likes to be told he is a sinner, it would be well for you to share with your students some wrong thing you have done (perhaps as a child)–something that proves you were a sinner. When students realize that their teacher has sinned, they will be less embarrassed to admit that they have sinned.

Seek to lead your students to the Lord Jesus who waits to cleanse each heart from sin.

Please study *all* the Scripture references in this lesson.

The *aim* of the lesson: To show the consequences of sin, that God hates sin and will punish sin.

What your students should *know*: The Lord Jesus loves them and died for them.

What your students should *feel*: The need to receive Jesus Christ as Saviour.

What your students should *do*:
Unsaved: Turn to the Lord Jesus in faith and receive Him as Saviour.
Saved: Witness to unsaved friends explaining that they can have eternal life by trusting in the Lord Jesus.

Lesson outline (for the teacher's and students' notebooks):
1. Sin is missing the mark (Romans 3:23).
2. Everyone has a sinful heart (Jeremiah 17:9-10).
3. Sin separates us from God (Ezekiel 18:4; Romans 6:23).
4. Jesus died for our sins (1 Corinthians 15:3-4).

The verse to be memorized:

For the wages of sin is death; but the gift of God is eternal life through Jesus Christ our Lord. (Romans 6:23)

THE LESSON

If you were to search through the whole world, you would not be able to find one person who has not done something wrong. Every boy and girl, every man and woman, has done wrong things. People who do wrong things are sinners. And since we all have done wrong things, we all are sinners!

1. SIN IS MISSING THE MARK
Romans 3:23

God is without sin. God is holy and free from wrong of any kind. "There is none holy as the LORD" (1 Samuel 2:2). He is above everyone. "The Lord is righteous in all His ways, and holy in all His works" (Psalm 145:17).

God has never thought a wrong thought. He has never done a wrong deed. He has never lied. He has never cheated. God is so pure and perfect that He turns away from sin. (See Habakkuk 1:13.) God hates the wrong things people do. He hates sin.

Show Illustration #13

What is sin? Sin is breaking the law of God. Sin is missing the mark of the perfection of God. Like the plank in the illustration which fails to bridge the chasm between earth and Heaven, we fall short of reaching God. "All have sinned and come short of the glory of God" (Romans 3:23). We may be very good, we may go to church, we may give money to the church. (See Isaiah 64:6.) But still we come short of reaching the perfection of God.

No matter how good we are and no matter how many good things we do, we can never get rid of sin by ourselves. What we *do*, however, is not as important as what we *are* in our hearts. And no one but God can see what our hearts are really like.

2. EVERYONE HAS A SINFUL HEART
Jeremiah 17:9-10

Show Illustration #14

God says that everyone has a sinful heart. (See Jeremiah 17:9-10.) This means that I have a sinful heart. It means you have a sinful heart. The dark heart in the illustration reminds us that people do wrong things. Often they sin when it is dark. (See John 3:19, 20.) They sin because they are sinners.

3. SIN SEPARATES US FROM GOD
Ezekiel 18:4; Romans 6:23

Remember the man who came to the Lord Jesus to be healed of his leprosy? Even if that man had only one spot, he had leprosy. So, too, if a person does only one wrong thing, he is a sinner. He is separated from God just as the one who does many wrong things is separated from Him.

Show Illustration #15

People with leprosy are separated from their friends and family. So, too, sin like a great wall separates the sinner from God.

A man sick with leprosy cannot get rid of his spots by himself. Covering his spots does not help. No matter what he tries to do, he still has leprosy. So a sinner cannot get rid of his sins by trying to cover them or by trying to be good. We can do nothing by ourselves to take away our sin. There is no human remedy for sin. Our sins separate us from God.

In two of our lessons (#2 and #3) we learned that sickness may sometimes be the result of sin. But the Lord Jesus is more concerned about a sinful heart than a sick body. If He healed a person of his sickness and did not forgive his sin, that person would receive the wages of sin: death–being forever separated from God and from all that is good and pure and holy.

How did sin start? You remember that Lucifer, the beautiful angel of God, was created perfect. (See New Testament, Volume 2, Lesson #4.) But one day Lucifer, instead of thinking about God and His holiness and worshiping Him, began thinking of himself. He thought proudly of his power. Then he decided he wanted to be like God. And that was sin. The very first sin was the sin of pride. Because of his sin, Lucifer lost much of his power. He lost his fine name and became known as *Satan,* or the *Devil.* (Read Ezekiel 28:12-15; Isaiah 14:12-15.)

How did sin come into the world? When God made the world, everything was good and right and perfect. (See Genesis 1:31.) The first man and woman, Adam and Eve, were without sin. They did only those things that were right and good. But one day Satan, in the form of a serpent, came into the beautiful garden. No one was afraid of serpents, for at that time there was nothing to fear. Everything was perfect. But Satan tempted Eve. He suggested that she disobey God. Eve listened to Satan. And Eve obeyed Satan. She ate some fruit from the one tree that had been forbidden by God. Then she gave some of the fruit to Adam to eat. (See Genesis 3:1-6.) They both chose their own way instead of God's way. They disobeyed God.

At that moment Adam and Eve became sinners. No longer were they the happy people they had been when God first made them. Sin had entered their hearts. They were sad.

Because the first people who lived sinned, all who have been born since Adam and Eve have been sinners. We are all born with sinful hearts. That is why we sin. But not only are we *born* sinners, we *choose* to sin. We choose our way against God's way. And that is sin.

God hates sin. He has to punish those who are sinners. When Lucifer sinned, he lost his high position. Sin separated Lucifer from God.

When Adam and Eve sinned they, too, were punished. They were sent out of a beautiful garden in which God had walked and talked with them. Their sin separated them from God. Because of their sin something else happened: they began to die. They did not die at once. But their bodies, instead of being the kind that would live forever, became the kind that would die. God has warned: "The soul that sinneth, it shall die" (Ezekiel 18:4). And: "The wages of sin is death" (Romans 6:23).

4. JESUS DIED FOR OUR SINS
1 Corinthians 15:3-4

Show Illustration #16

But far worse than the death of the body is the final punishment for sin: separation from God forever. Satan will receive that punishment. And so will all those who refuse to believe in the Lord Jesus and who do not receive Him as Saviour. The unforgiven sinner will be forever in a place of torment. (See John 8:24.)

When the Lord Jesus died on the cross, He died for our sins so that we need no longer be separated from God. Those whose hearts have been cleansed by believing on the Lord Jesus and receiving Him as Saviour have eternal life. They will be forever with God in His beautiful home, Heaven.

Have *you* chosen the wages of sin or the gift of God? The Lord Jesus loves you. He died for you. He waits for you to receive Him.

NOTE TO THE TEACHER

Please pray that the Holy Spirit will convict each one you teach. Ask Him to cause the unsaved to turn to the Lord Jesus in faith and receive Him as Saviour. Pray, too, that the Christian students will be challenged to witness to their unsaved friends concerning eternal life in the Lord Jesus.

www.ingramcontent.com/pod-product-compliance
Lightning Source LLC
Chambersburg PA
CBHW060807090426
42736CB00002B/190